UNSPOKEN

UNSPOKEN

NEVER UNDERESTIMATE THE POWER OF SILENCE

ASHINI GUNARATNE

authorHOUSE®

AuthorHouse™
1663 Liberty Drive
Bloomington, IN 47403
www.authorhouse.com
Phone: 1-800-839-8640

Published by AuthorHouse   04/04/2012

ISBN: 978-1-4685-4830-3 (sc)
ISBN: 978-1-4685-4829-7 (e)

*Dedicated to my parents, my family, my friends
and the two best schools ever (so far)
P.S.22 and P.S.861 ☺
And for M.P who asked for me to right this here ☺*

INTRODUCTION

What side will you choose? Do you know what I'm talking about? Well . . . Do you? Probably not, but that's okay. You aren't here to be tested on what you know; it's what you shouldn't know that really matters. It's serious and confidential but I'm still going to tell you but remember just in case if anyone asks you didn't hear it from me.

REMEMBER TO STAY UNSPOKEN
. . . SHHHH . . .
NEVER UNDERESTIMATE THE POWER OF
SILENCE

CHAPTER ONE

Her name was Hope. You probably think she sounds like she's a nice and sweet person, don't you? Guess again. She was a twelve year old mystery. She has tan color skin and straight black hair. Her eyes tell you everything but nothing. They're black not dark brown, but black. No one believes it but it's true. Some say she's cold blooded and you never know, maybe she is. Hope is a dark soul. A lost dark soul: just waiting for the truth to finally come, *if* it decides to come at all. When it comes to Hope, mortality means nothing. Immortality means everything, and life? Well life is a question that should stay unanswered.

Hope is different than everyone else. She's the odd one, the outcast from her family. Hope isn't just one of those people, who are just different in their own way, that definition goes for just about everyone. Hope wasn't like not human different either, it's just that she had different thoughts and dreams that just made her well . . . different. She was the outsider to everyone else and the outsider stays unspoken. Ever since she was little she wasn't interested in all the things those other children liked. They would go play hopscotch and jump rope but not Hope. Hope would sit at home at draw things with her special black crayon. It was special because the company it was made from was called Hope. Hope was little at the time and thought it was named after her and that's why the colors weren't so bright and cheery. It still doesn't really make sense to me because the colors aren't bright and cheery and the full name of the company was really called <u>HOPE FOR IMAGINATION</u>. Strange . . .

Hope had a friend her name was Destiny. Destiny was an inch taller than Hope; she had brown eyes and wavy short dark brown hair. People often thought Hope and Destiny were sisters because some thought that they sort of looked a like in some ways, but people usually thought they were sisters because of their names. They lived across the street from each other for about seven years now. That's how they met, their mothers set them up on a play date and they've been friends since, from what I told you it's probably hard to think that Hope would have a friend but she did. Both Hope and Destiny go to the same middle school but they were in two different classes. Bummer.

And who am I you ask? Well I'm her teller. That's what my kind is called, Tellers. I tell the story of Hope. No I'm not her stalker, I'm the writer. I write her life story. Everyone already has a second person inside of them, we're on the outside. You'll figure out more as you go. Follow the clues and it will show. Dreams do end in the morning but don't forget, they begin at night.

One day Hope went to class. She was a little late. Hope had a late slip and pen in one hand and in the other hand was a book and her homework. Her book bag was wide open. All of sudden her books fell out of her bag. Luckily she made it to her seat before they came toppling out. Hopes seat was in the front right corner of the classroom. Her books falling didn't really catch anyone's attention; no one really cared about what was going on with Hope, except Ms. Beatrico. Ms. Beatrico was a tall, light skinned, perky teacher. Sometimes people thought she had nothing better to do than text random people in her contact list who just won't reply back. She was still in her late twenties. To me it seemed like she saw something in Hope, something others can't.

Ms. Beatrico came over to help Hope pick up her books. Hope's writer's notebook was opened to a certain page already when Ms. Beatrico picked it up. Coincidence? She looked at the page. There was a poem on it, Ms. Beatrico was curious about the poem after the she read the title. So she started to read it, she was a fast reader. "Hope, did you write this?" asked Ms. Beatrico. Hope looked at the page.

"Yea—I mean yes, I did" she replied. Hope corrected her yea into yes because Ms. Beatrico is very serious about her grammar. Students respected this because there were very few things Ms. Beatrico was serious about.

"It's very good"

"Thank you"

"Would you like to read it in front of the class?"

"Um . . . Sure"

Hope really didn't want to read it, but if she didn't Ms. Beatrico would read it and she wouldn't read it right. She would read it in a happy voice and Hope didn't mean for this to be a happy poem. She never means for her writing to be happy, except in kindergarten when she had to write about something happy that happened to her. Right when Hope was about to recite her poem the morning announcements came on. They started the pledge of allegiance.

. . . With liberty and justice for all

They ended the morning announcements a minute or two later. The announcements said all the usual boring stuff, that wasn't too fun, the only difference today was that the school nurse was absent, how exciting . . . "Class settle down Hope would like to share something with you" said Ms. Beatrico. Hope thought to herself, *well I don't want to do it; I'm just going to do it.*

Hope came up to the front of the classroom. She looked up so she could get a glance of the faces she'd be reading too. She didn't like most of those faces, she actually hated some of those faces. They didn't like her very much either. It was like Batman was having a cup of coffee with the Joker. Hope looked back down at her book and took a deep breath. She removed the black locks flowing into her face to behind her ear. Hope cleared her throat and then she began to read her poem

Unspoken
Surrounding life's ways
Follows me throughout my days
Means everything
Means nothing
Unspoken
Believe in everything
Believe in nothing

Unspoken
Through death and tears
Through life's fears
It all goes away
Nothing is ever to stay
Unspoken

Some kid in the back row shouted out "Wow she can talk! And it's kind of selfish to write a poem about yourself" He was referring to her quietness and that made a few people laughed at the joke, others clapped lightly for the poem.

"Well at least I can get my food into my mouth." Replied Hope referring to the stain on his shirt. That got a few giggles too from the people who understood what she was talking about, others just looked confused as they always do. Hope made a face at the kid with the rude comment and went back to her seat. Ms. Beatrico clapped and went to her desk in the back of the classroom and as usual checked her phone for any messages. Her teller must be really sad and without friends if she makes her person have no social life.

A lot of the kids in Hopes class didn't like her. They always called her names and talked about her. "Look at what she's wearing." Some girls would say. "I heard she wears black all the time because she can't afford clothes with color and she hides that with that whole gothic thing" said others. Hope knew about the rumors but she didn't say anything to stop them, but it was the reason for her tears. The tears that make her pillow damp every night. No one really understood Hope, sometimes not even her parents really understood her.

Meanwhile, Destiny was in her classroom two doors down from Hope's classroom. She was reading a book, a huge book. It was a realistic-fiction book and based on the look on Destiny's face, it was very interesting. Destiny's teacher was a few years older than Ms. Beatrico so she was about thirty. No one really knew for sure, she wouldn't tell anyone but she looked like she was in her early thirties, maybe even 29. Her name was Ms. S. Ms. S was actually a pretty fun teacher compared to Ms. Beatrico who went a little wacky at times. Ms. S gave more homework though. Destiny hated how much homework she gives out.

Later on was lunch. The food was disgusting. Hope got macaroni and it looked a bit under-cooked. Destiny got a roast beef sandwich and it was really cold. "You know at first I thought disgusting middle school lunch was just a stereotype. I was wrong" said Hope actually sounding like a normal happy kid for once. She thought she could do that with Destiny.

"I know right?" Destiny replied. She said it with a small giggle.

"Yeah, anyways before we get into a whole conversation about gross food the most horrible thing happened to me in homeroom" said Hope.

"What?" asked Destiny.

"I had to read in front of the class, like I had to stand in the front of the room and everything."

"Read what?"

"A poem I wrote"

"And . . . what's so bad about that?" asked Destiny casually.

"You say it as if you read in front of the class everyday Ms. I hate reading out loud" said Hope with her arms crossed.

"True." Replied Destiny realizing Hope was right.

After school when the girls went home Hope did her homework and then she began to sketch a picture. It was a picture of everything and nothing. Everything that was in that picture was something but in the real world it was truly nothing. Hope felt as if she should be in that picture, she felt as though it was the same concept for her. She heard a knock on the door. "Come in" Said Hope. It was her little brother. He was four years old and everyone called him Little J.J. He was named after his dad, Joseph and his grandfather Jerry. So his name was Jerry Joseph. Hope was named after her great grandmother on her mother's side. Little J.J held up ten fingers and said

"Mommy said dinner is in ten minwuts" He was little and still couldn't pronounce minutes or most words with the letter r in it.

"Okay tell mom I'll be down in ten miwuts" Hope mocked her little brothers' word pronunciation. He nodded and ran down the steps then 30 seconds later ran back up and into Hopes room.

"Sissy, can I have one of your pictures?" asked Little J.J. Hope looked down at her drawing and said

"Why . . . ?" She know didn't if she should be elated or not. You never really know what little kids are going to do with your stuff.

"I'll give it back . . . there's this girl at shool and she's aways saying how her sissy can draw so good but the pictuwes she brings in are ugly I want to show them yowr art . . . please . . ." Hope giggled at how her brother pronounced some words.

"Okay" she said "But don't ruin it okay?"

"O-K!"

"Alright you can pick a picture from my wall." Little J.J carefully looked at every picture. Hope giggled again when he held his chin and looked closely into the detail of each drawing. Finally he said

"That one!" Hope brought her chair over to the wall. Little J.J picked a picture that was all the way at the top. She got it down for him. Hope looked at this picture for a second and thought that he picked a nice looking picture. Hope handed the picture to Little J.J, he ran away into his room across the hall with her picture. Dinner came and their mom cooked a nice warm meal. Little J.J told their parents about the drawing. Hopes parents didn't really pay attention to anything irrelevant happening in theirs or anyone else's life. Little J.J understood this but he kept talking about it to their parents. Everyone always giggled when he miss pronounced a word.

"Hope how was your day?" asked Hope's mom.

"The usual" replied Hope picking out the peppers from her mom's special salad.

"So . . . not very good?" asked her father. "Not good" or "Horrible" was Hopes usual response.

"Well it wasn't too bad . . . this morning wasn't very good though I had to read a poem in front of the whole class" said Hope.

"What poem? Do I know it?" asked her mother curiously.

"No it's, it's a poem I wrote" Replied Hope unsure of what her mother's response might be.

"I'd love to read it after dinner" she said.

"Okay" said Hope. After dinner Hope went up to her room and got her notebook and went to her parents' room. Her dad was working on the computer and her mom was reading a book. "I have my poem" she said

"That's nice sweetie, show your mother I'm working right now.

"Um . . . okay" said Hope and she walked over to her mother who was lying down on the bed. "Mom I have the poem you wanted to-"

"Shhh" her mother cut her off "I'm trying to find out who the murderer is, go show your father."

"But I-"

"Shhh!" Hope walked out of the room as a single tear ran down her cheek. Hope saw her little brother in the hallway.

"Sissy?" He asked.

"Yea" answered Hope.

"I'd like to here your poem"

"Umm ok" They walked to little J.J's room. Hope tucked her little brother into bed and sat by him on the small blue chair. Then she began to read her poem.

꧁꧂

CHAPTER TWO

L ater on that day Hope had a dream. It felt like as soon
as she closed her eyes to go to sleep she was imported
to a whole other dimension within a blink. She didn't know
where she was. It was foggy and the sky was a pitch black.
There was not a single star shining and the moon was lost in
space. She didn't know if she was in a dream or not. Hope
didn't waste her time trying to figure it out. Remember she's
not a happy person, sometimes just being with her a day
can change your point of view.

Hope started to walk to her left. She could barely see
where she was going. Hope tripped on something and fell
to a damp ground. She managed to pull herself up only
to realize a frog was on top of her head. She had a dark
soul but Hope wouldn't dare hurt an innocent creature,
I guess her soul isn't that dark after all. The fog cleared
up gradually and Hope was finally able to see where
she was going. She called out; "HELLO?" there was no
answer. "HELLO?" she called out again, this time she
heard something. What she heard was a familiar voice,
the voice said,

"Hope? Is that you?" Hope tried to find out where the sound came from, and then it came again but louder, "HOPE?" Hope finally saw a faint silhouette of what looked like a person. She walked over and saw the person. She wasn't scared, Hope tapped the person on the shoulder. The person jumped with fright of who just touched them. They finally saw each other face to face it was Destiny. Destiny was in her pajamas and she looked scared to death but only for a few seconds.

"Oh hey Hope what's up?" asked Destiny casually as if they were in the school cafeteria and happened to see each other.

"Umm Destiny why are you acting so casual?" asked Hope.

"Because, I'm freaking out on the inside!" said Destiny changing the tone of her normal voice to a high pitched voice. A slightly heavy wind came. All of a sudden lightning struck and Hope was gone, Hope looked around for Destiny but couldn't find her. Hope felt as though she was trapped. Then there came a sound. It sounded almost like a drum but whoever was playing it played it very slowly. Destiny was alone. "Hope? Where'd you go?" called out Destiny. There was no answer. She called out again, "Hope stop playing where are you?" Once again there was no answer. Then something grabbed Destiny's shoulder from behind. Destiny said, "Glad I found you Hope" and turned around.

When Destiny turned around, she saw that it wasn't Hope who had grasped her shoulder. It was someone else, something else. "YOU'RE—YOU'RE—YOU'RE not Hope" Destiny couldn't speak she was scared. Standing in front of her was a tall thing. It had golden locks flowing from its skull and fingernails sharp enough to pierce through skin. Her nails weren't the only thing that could pierce through skin, she had luminous white fangs.

Destiny wanted to scream but she couldn't. It was as if she became a mute and even if the tried to speak not a living soul will hear her. Destiny sprinted but she knew she couldn't outrun a vampire. She decided to hide. It was too hard to see where she was going. Destiny remained quiet as she ran so the vampire couldn't find where she was going. Destiny hid behind a bush. Then all of a sudden that lightning came again. Destiny heard someone step on a fallen branch. The sounds of footsteps were getting louder and louder. Destiny panicked as she didn't know what to do. The footsteps were getting closer. Destiny covered herself in fallen branches and leaves. She looked around but could barely see. The sounds were louder now. What he didn't know was that anyone who would look that way could see that there was someone on the floor. Destiny laid on the ground hoping whoever it was would pass by, but then she opened her eyes and saw feet. Destiny remained quiet, her eyes moved up and saw a hand coming towards her, but this hand wasn't very big. The hand picked up some leaves and then Destiny saw the face.

"Destiny? What are you doing?" the face was Hopes face. Destiny got up and looked around.

"Hope, where did you go?" asked Destiny cautious for the vampire.

"I, I don't know" Hope was confused, Destiny was bewildered by her answer. Then they both her a voice coming from the sky, it repeated

"Hope! Hope! Hope!" Hope woke up only to see that voice coming from the sky was her mother telling her to wake up. Hope looked up at the clock it was 6:45. School started at 8:00. Hope got ready to go and left.

CHAPTER THREE

"It felt so real" said Hope to Destiny. They were sitting in the cafeteria together during lunch.

"Wait did a blonde vampire with long nails chase me?" asked Destiny. She knew about how the vampire looked without Hope even telling her. Hope took a bite out of her sandwich and asked

"Yea . . . but how do you-"

"I had that dream to" They both looked super confused, I've been working on making that face for her. "Did you disappear before the vampire came but then when I hid you came back?"

"Yea . . . Did lightning come before I disappear and were you covering yourself with what was on the floor when you were hiding?"

"Yea . . . Was I like not able to speak a word when I got scared?"

"Yea was it like foggy and the sky was pitch black?"

"Yea" said Destiny both interested in the conversation and at the same time very scared. Hope started to get a weird feeling about this whole thing and that was because I felt weird about it. She put her lunch aside and just drank some juice. The two girls spent their lunch period asking each other questions about their dreams. The two dreams seemed to be exactly alike.

Hope was thinking during math *how can we possibly have the same exact dream? How can something like that ever happen to anyone besides in the movies or on TV. ?Life gets harder when it's so weird* "Hope?", called Mr. Udensi the math teacher. Hope wasn't paying attention; she looked at the board trying to find which question they were on. She bit her lip and asked

"Can you please repeat the question, sir?" She added in the sir hoping he wouldn't be mad at her. A girl in their class giggled.

"Certainly Hope. What is this answer when b=4 and a=2?" Hope looked at the problem, it was. Hope started to do the problem in her notebook. The entire class including Mr. Udensi stared at her, Hope hated when people stared at her so she just blurted out

"3!"

"Can anyone help Hope?" asked Mr. Udensi. The girl who giggled before shot up her hand. "Yes Mindy" Mindy didn't like Hope either. Hope saw her as a big threat how she's always trying to make her cry. Mindy smiled and said

"The answer is 64"

"Very good" said Mr. Udensi "Hope do you understand why the answer is 64?" Hope felt embarrassed but the stares were back and she just said

"Yes"

Later on that day Hope was doing homework then she heard a sound. *Rib bit! Rib bit!*

Hope looked out her window and she saw the frog that had been in her dream when she fell. She thought it was just a coincidence. The frog went away after a minute. The noise was gone and Hope continued her homework as if nothing suspicious was going on.

I think something's going on. I told you I tell her story but her story is changing. Sometimes change is good, when it's not bad. Look out Hope. I didn't put that frog there so who did? They're not supposed to be interfering with some one else's story.

Destiny came over after Hope finished her homework. "So what do you thinks going on?" asked Destiny. She walked in and sat on the bed while eating an apple, Hope sitting on the floor.

"About . . ." replied Hope knowing what Destiny was talking about but not wanting to talk about it. Normally I'd make Hope like this stuff but if Destiny had the same exact dream then someone copied off my writing, now I have to find out why . . .

"Oh like you don't know" Hope had an expression on her face that showed that she really had know idea what Destiny was talking about. "The dream!" exclaimed Destiny taking another bite out of her apple.

"Oh the dream . . . right I forgot about that for a second" Hope really didn't forget but something about this whole dream thing made her feel sick to her stomach and that usually doesn't happen to Hope.

"Oh my gosh! How could you forget it?!?!" Destiny was practically screaming at Hope. "We have to figure it out, grab one of your magic books or potions or whatever! This will be like in the movies!" Destiny actually seemed happy unlike Hope who kept telling herself this was a dream so that she can wake up and feel okay . . . But it wasn't a dream, it was worse, it was real life.

"How would a spell book help us?" asked Hope and yes she had a spell book but it was one the she order from an online bookstore. I don't think its going to work but that's my choice anyways, I decide what happens in her life.

"I don't know maybe we'll find a spell that'll tell us what's going on, now get it! Get it!" Destiny smiled with enthusiasm, she was so excited her apple fell out of her hand and hit Hope on the head. Hope just looked at Destiny for a second then she went to go get the book from her bookshelf. Hope placed the book on the floor in between her and Destiny. Hope got the key from her drawer and unlocked the book. Destiny flipped to the table of contents. "Wanna try the dream spells?" asked Destiny.

"It's worth a shot" said Hope and flipped to that page.

"Here it says there's a spell that could explain your dream" said Destiny.

"A therapist will do the same thing" replied Hope ruining Destiny's happiness. She said it with kind of an attitude. "Blood will help us more than a spell and nothing will solve everything."

"Why are you acting like this don't you want to figure this out? This is like an adventure like in the movies"

"Movies are full of green screens and sound effects! They're not real!"

"You always want everything that'll never happen to happen! When have you wanted anything to be real?" Destiny was getting angry.

"When everything started to become fake!" Yelled Hope.

"Are you crazy, are you like bipolar or something? Nothing is becoming fake!" Destiny was changing colors.

"How do you know your blind!"

"Now you're being really crazy I have 20/20 vision!"

"Your blind to everything and nothing!"

"When am I going to stop hearing about everything thing and nothing? What's your favorite color? Everything and nothing. Ugh! Everything and nothing this everything and nothing that! Make up your mind!"

"You don't get it!"

"What does that even mean? Wait I don't care" Destiny paused "Will you just—let's just try to figure this out ok?" She definitely did not want to start a fight with Hope. They've never fought before, I mean they've had disagreements but never any fights, and no I don't mean fist fights for all you violent people out there.

"Okay, whatever" Hope didn't want to fight either. "But can we do it tomorrow my head kind of hurts?"

"Okay sure!" Said Destiny "Well bye!" and she left.

Finally she's gone! Destiny belongs to another teller and she was interfering with my writing for Hope. I don't like what's going on, someone copied my work. I don't want to confront them, see we tellers don't really like each other very much and that's because tellers envy each other, just saying something smart in front of someone else could make a teller feel foolish and think: "Destiny's teller did something different, her teller copied what I wrote now I will get my revenge but for now I have to finish writing for Hope.

That night Little J.J came in to return Hopes picture. "Thank Ywo Sissy!" said Little J.J and he hugged her.

"You're Welcome" Said Hope "How did the girl react when she saw this drawing?"

"She said it was pretty but her sissy could do better, but twen she said to her fwiend that your pictuwe wa bettew" He said as he giggled. Hope giggled too. I'm not in the mood to make her sad and depressed right now so her dark sides going to be taking a break while I plan my revenge . . .

CHAPTER FOUR

That night Hope fell asleep easily, when the teller isn't there for their person, the person goes unconscious but I just made her fall asleep. I had to go to see Destiny's teller and have a little chat but it can't be too long I have to come back to Hope.

So I got there, I rang the doorbell but still no answer. "HELLO IN THERE!!! THIS IS HOPES TELLER! I NEED TO TALK TO YOUUUUU!!!" I shouted. I started coughing but then I heard the back door slam shut, I ran across to the back where Destiny's teller was trying to escape. She knew why I was here. I managed to catch her before she got a way.

"What do you want?" She yelled.

"Like you don't know" I answered. I was holding on to the hood of her jacket she tried to escape but then she just took off the jacket. I knew she was about to run and he did but I didn't chase her, I hid. She ran around the corner of the house then looked back. I watched discreetly. She looked around and didn't see me. Her name was Teller #19997124, this number represented Destiny it has her birthday on it and it says that she was the fourth person born on that day, I just call her DT its short for Destiny's teller. I'm teller #19998042, I'm also about to hurt someone. DT was coming back inside I hid on beside of the door. Then she walked in and I jumped on her putting all my weight on her to hold her down. DT put up her hands and said

"You caught me, I'll talk!"

"Excellent" I said with a grin. "Now why did you copy my work?

"I had an idea" there was a pause.

"Well . . . what was it?" I asked. I was actually curious.

"We don't have to work"

"Our person has to pass away for us to retire! Everyone knows that!"

"Or it's the other way around." She smiled, I had a bad feeling about this.

"What are you talking about?" My tone changed, I was nervous.

"If our people don't have us they can retire from life."

"But that's only if we pass awa-" I gulped suddenly I noticed she was holding a knife in her right hand. I took a small step back and she took a big step closer. "Think before you do!"

"Oh I thought about it ever since our fight ten years ago!" She had anger in her eyes as she stood there staring at me. I thought for a second and then I knew what she was talking about. Ten years I had to decide what kind of person I wanted Hope to be. DT gave me a lot of ideas then she told me to make her a fun, upbeat, sporty, and really nice girl, and I did sort of the opposite. DT got mad at mad at me and she swore that she'd hate me forever, I was confused at first at why she wanted to make Hope and Destiny best friends if she hated me but now I understand. She wanted to find the right time to copy my work and give it to Destiny, Hopes dream was an opportunity. Then she knew I was going to come and when I came she had the chance to kill me, then with me gone Hope s gone too. She planned all of this because Hope didn't come out to be the way she wanted, Hope came out as the way I wanted. The back door was still open, I ran out when DT least expected it. She froze for a sec and by the time that she realized that now she had to catch me I covered a lot of ground. She hollered something at me but I couldn't make out the words.

I got back to Hope. She was still sleeping, no dreams, no anything, so I had time to write. I wrote a new dream for tomorrow and I kept Destiny out of it. I had enough time to write her life all the way to next weekend. Now that what I had to do was done I had the chance to torture DT by making Hope even more dark than she was before. But the question is did I really end the problem that I'm claiming to have solved?

The next morning Hope avoided Destiny. I bugged DT by having Hope wear all black. Hope walked to class alone today and she walked faster when she saw Destiny walking over to her. Hope felt the normal way she felt most of the time: alone. Ms. Beatrico watched Hope as she wrote in her book during homeroom. "Whatcha writing there Hope?" asked Ms. Beatrico in her normally peppy voice. Hope looked up at her, her eyes were red and it showed that she was crying.

"Nothing." She said and she looked back down at her book as another tear drop fell down leading the writing to smear.

"Hope, what's the matter? Why are you crying?" Ms. Beatrico no longer used her peppy voice, now she sounded concerned. She really was a good person but no one really accepted her as that, they all just thought of her as the goofy teacher that all the other teachers talked about behind her back.

"Life leaves teardrops on death."

"Did someone die Hope?" asked Ms. Beatrico sounding worried and holding her hand to her heart.

"No but someone will, I can feel it." I couldn't believe what I was doing. I was thinking about what happened with DT when I was writing and the feeling I had went to Hope, that's why she's feeling this way inside. I can't control her feelings when they've gone to her already because she has memories and memories will bring back the feelings, memories are in her heart and I control only the brain.

"Hope do you need to see the guidance counselor? I can call her now."

"No thank you, pain is nothing to express. Pain is a scar and feelings are what goes away."

"But isn't pain a feeling?" asked a kid listening to the conversation.

"Mind your own business." Said Ms. Beatrico, "But isn't pain a feeling?" I giggled since she repeated the kid's question.

"Pain is much, much more than just a feeling." Answered Hope, her face looked like it had stripes since her tears came down and wet her face.

"I think you do need to see the guidance counselor, Hope."

"You're the teacher." Replied Hope. She didn't sounding happy or excited about it at all. Going to the guidance counselor wasn't the most fun thing to do. Hope had to go during lunch, at least it helped her avoid Destiny. So now Hope can see what's going to happen and that's not good. She has the feeling of death and she shouldn't. It's sort of my fault I guess for thinking about it but DT is too old to be holding a grudge over something so small, okay it's a person's personality and lifestyle choices, that isn't small but still she doesn't have to hold a grudge. I made Hope the way I want and DT made Destiny the way that she wants. I thought there would be peace between us but no. Now Hope partially knows something she shouldn't.

So later on Hope was walking down to get her lunch then she would go to the guidance counselor. Destiny spotted Hope in the cafeteria. "Hey! Hope!" She called out. Hope turned around and continued walking as if she didn't see Destiny. Destiny caught up and grabbed Hope by the arm. "Hope, why are you ignoring me today?" asked Destiny. She almost seemed upset but I saw right through her.

"I'm not ignoring you" Answered Hope, she had no expression on her face.

"Then let's go have some artificial school lunch." Destiny was all happy and peppy now.

"I . . . I can't"

"Why not if you want to sit with someone else I'll come to" Destiny didn't want to sit with someone else but she was willing to.

"Ms. Beatrico scheduled me an appointment with the guidance counselor."

"Oh, well do you want me to come?" I see what's going on DT wants to know some more bot Hope so that she could somehow use it against me, good thing she doesn't know any of Hopes secrets and only Destiny does. For tellers when their person hears secret they don't hear it, it's basically the same thing as watching someone whisper something to someone else, you see it but you don't hear it.

"No it's fine, I'll go alone" I made Hope quiet for a reason and Destiny won't go away, see when people have a conversation we have to write right at that moment unless the tellers meet before and discuss what they would say.

"All right" said Destiny and she left. Hope went the other way. The guidance counselor or as I like to call her "Ms. Crazy is good" had a super colorful office, it made Hope sick. Then Hope turned right to sit in the waiting room and was shocked to see Destiny there eating a bologna sandwich.

"What are you doing here?" asked Hope not happy to see Destiny.

"I had something to tell the guidance counselor." Answered Destiny with smile.

"Oh, well okay." Hope sat down across from Destiny. They didn't really talk to each other that much. Both of them just sat there quietly eating their lunches and dinking their juices. Then Ms. Crazy Is Good opened the door and came out. Her real name was Ms. C and I think that C stands for Crazy Is Good. She waved good bye to a little girl who ran out crying.

"Hope!" She called out. Hope threw out her tray and walked in to the room. Destiny followed Hope into the room and Hope looked at Destiny with *why are you here?* Look. The room was full of rainbows and sunshine. YUCK! "Would you like some candy" asked Ms. C holding out a jar full of various candies towards Hope. Hope took out a piece of gum.

"Umm Destiny? What are you doing here?" asked Hope.

"I was about to ask the same thing" said Ms. C "Destiny this session is for Hope only sorry but you're next." Destiny looked at Hope and left. Ms. C looked at a notepad and flipped over a few pages

"Okay Hope, Ms. Beatrico told me you were talking about death and you were crying during homeroom, what happened?"

"Everything and nothing." Answered Hope.

"I'm sorry?" Ms. C only got one answer from Hope and was already confused.

"Everything happened but everything is nothing and vice versa"

"Okay . . . and what is everything?"

"Nothing." Ms. C took off her glasses.

"Hope what are you talking about?"

"Everything and Nothing." Ms. C drank some water after taking a deep breathe.

"Hope what does that mean? And don't say everything and nothing." She sounded frustrated.

"It means nothing but nothing is everything and everything is nothing." Answered Hope.

"Hope, I'm trying to help you please cooperate with me." Hope nodded. "Okay so what is wrong?"

"Everything" answered Hope.

"And what's everything? Is it family troubles, school troubles, or what?" Asked Ms. C, she was starting to calm down.

"Everything is nothing." Answered Hope. I enjoy this conversation, you would die laughing if you saw this in person.

"Hope you're not helping"

"Neither are you" Replied Hope.

"Don't you talk back to me!" yelled Ms. C. I don't think anyone has ever annoyed her, this much at school. Ms. C wrote something on a slip of paper. "Come back tomorrow during homeroom" Hope walked out of the room to see a pile of kids piled around the door. Ms. C called in Destiny. A girl and a boy stopped her.

"What'd you do to her" asked the boy.

"Everything." Answered Hope.

"And what's everything?" asked the girl.

"Nothing" said Hope and she walked away. I'm still laughing. Everything is nothing and nothing is everything! Hilarious! Ms. C must think that Hope has some serious problems from the way she was talking.

ꏗ

CHAPTER FIVE

That day when Hope got home her mom was in the kitchen. She was making brownies with little J.J. He had chocolate all over his face and was eating chocolate chips as Hope walked in. Their mom was popping some chocolate chips into her mouth herself. Hope grabbed a juice pouch and went upstairs to her room. She found Destiny waiting there. Destiny was on Hope's computer reading a short story Hope wrote. Hope ran in and x' out of the document when she saw what Destiny was reading.

"Why were you reading that?" Shouted Hope pointing to her screen which was now blank.

"Calm down." Said Destiny with her hands up in front of her. "I was just reading." Hope looked at her wall and all of her picture were taken down.

"What happened to my pictures?"

"I just wanted to see them" exclaimed Destiny.

"You didn't have to take them down to see them!" Shouted Hope. Wait a minute, were Hope and Destiny having a *real* fight? I think they were, Oh My Goodness! Hope and Destiny were actually on the verge of ripping each other's hair out and it's even better because I can make Hope do that. This is exciting.

"I took them down because I couldn't see the ones on top!" replied Destiny.

"Then you should have stood on a chair, it's what you did when you took them down isn't it?" yelled Hope pointing to the chair at her computer desk "Or you could have moved back and you didn't have to take down the pictures at the bottom!"

"It didn't look right if I took down the ones on the top and not the bottom!" shouted Destiny.

"That's so stupid!" It really was, I mean you have to admit it really was, DT do well during fights like talking back and stuff, which is one of the reasons why Hope nd Destiny never had a fight Destiny looked at Hopes face for a good 20 seconds. It was so quiet.

"Are you calling me stupid?" asked Destiny. There was no more shouting left but Destiny's face was red. Hope was silence at first but then she said

"I don't know . . . Maybe I am" Destiny's eyes were watery.

"Fine! Whatever." Said Destiny, she started off screaming but ended in a quiet voice. Destiny was really upset and she ran out of the room. Hope shut the door and looked out the window, Destiny was running across the street to her house. Then Hope started to take the pictures and stick them back on to her wall.

Around five o' clock Hope was still putting up pictures. She'd been doing it for about a little less than an hour, she was up to the top now and was standing on a chair. Her mom came into the room, she was wearing a teal dress that complimented her blue eyes. "Hope?" she asked.

"Yea?" answered Hope.

"Your father and I are going dancing with the Peters' as soon as your Aunt Tecla comes okay?" Hope didn't really like her aunt Tecla, she always went too crazy and didn't follow the rules. She always tried, like most immature adults to act younger than they really are. I wouldn't even be surprised if she took a nap while baking and started a fire.

"All right" said Hope, her mother was putting on pink earrings that actually did match.

"And I wanted to ask, why did Destiny run out crying earlier?"

"You don't care" answered Hope sitting down on her bed.

"Oh sweety I do care" relied her mother sitting down next to her.

"No you don't. I *know* you don't, and it's okay, I've been used to it for a while now.

"Honey! It's time to go!" called Hope's father as he was coming up the stair to say goodbye.

"We'll talk about this later." Said her mom and she gave Hope a kiss on the forehead. Then Hopes dad came in and did the same. Hope managed to finish putting up the rest of her pictures on her wall in five minutes. Hope decided to rest for a little while and watch some T.V but then Aunt Tecla walked in with Little J.J on her back.

"C'mon Hope lets make some cookies!" Said Aunt Tecla.

"Should a women your age really be carrying around a child on her back?" asked Hope. Aunt Tecla put down Little J.J and put her hands on her hips then asked

"and what's that supposed to mean?" Hope smiled.

"Nothing but nothing is everything and everything is nothing." She answered. Aunt Tecla and Little J.J looked at each other and yelled

"HUH?"

"Well Hope we'll be downstairs if you want to have some fun." Said Aunt Tecla then she and Little J.J went to the kitchen. There wasn't much to watch on T.V, just a bunch of reruns. Hope decided to take nap mostly because I was really tired. I did a lot of on the spot writing today, Hope had a lot of people to talk to.

I woke up an hour later and woke Hope up to. She smelt smoke, I told you that women might be the cause of a fire starting. Hope went downstairs, she rolled her eyes when she saw Aunt Tecla taking a nap with Little J.J curled up next to her. What did I tell, I said I wouldn't be surprised if that happened and it happened! Hope went into the kitchen and there wasn't a fire, the smoke was coming from the stove because the cookies were burnt. She woke up Aunt Tecla.

"Oopsies!" said Aunt Tecla with a giggle, "I guess I dozed off a little and forgot about the cookies, I'll clean this up you can go upstairs." Aunt Tecla took care of it, Little J.J woke up to the noise and helped too while Hope went back upstairs. It's kind of scary because Little J.J goes to Aunt Tecla's house every weekend while his parents go to work and Hope goes to Destiny's house.

Later on that day around 9 was when her parents came home. They seemed to have had lot of fun. After they got cleaned up and in their pajamas Hope knocked on the door and came in.

"Mom, you still want to talk to me about what happened with Destiny?" asked Hope.

"We talked about Destiny? When?" answered Hope's mom. Oh my gosh can't she be a little considerate and at least remember what they talked about? Hope stood by the door and held her wrist.

"Yea and you wanted to talk about me saying you don't care . . . ring a bell?"

"Oh you love me I love you, it's all good" replied her mother with a smile. It really wasn't something to smile about, I mean even though Hope said the things she said to her mom during their conversation, she as really happy to at least be talking to her mom. Hope looked and talked like she didn't care about being independent towards her parents but really she did care, she wanted what the other kids had from their parents. Hope turned around and walked towards her room.

"I knew she didn't care." Said Hope to herself. That was really sad. The least she could do was at least remember the conversation but she didn't even do that. I wonder if Hopes mom really didn't care about Hope. Maybe she loves her but she just can't take the time to do enough for her kids. We tellers didn't have parents. We were just born everytime a human is born, that's why baby's can't do much, we get trained for the first few years of our life then we get to write the story of the person who was born and gave us life.

CHAPTER SIX

That night Hope had another dream, I wrote it for her yesterday. Like I said Destiny wasn't in this one, but then I heard a ring, it was my phone. I answered it and I heard the cold voice of DT. "Hi there" She said "Have you gone through the dream you wrote yet?"

"No, why?" I asked. Wait how did she know I wrote a dream for Hope.

"I made a few changes." I ran to my book and saw that she put Destiny in the dream. I got an eraser but then DT said "Don't try to erase it, I used pen" We weren't allowed to use pen in our books unless we were retracing faded words from the past. With pen you can't erase so if a person comes up to talk to your person and you didn't plan it and you wrote in pen, then your person would just be standing there continuing to do what you wrote. The humans have a thing called white out and they have erasable pens, we should have those.

"When did you do this?" I asked.

"During your little nap" answered DT "And by the way, you snore in your sleep" and she hung up. Oh Squash! First she copies what I wrote and now she tampers with it? How rude! Let's just see what happens in DT's dream.

It didn't look too different, I saw Hope and she was inside a dark room with only one light. The light was shining towards the end of the room. The room Hope as in was long and narrow. She was just standing there confused and in shock not knowing what was going on until someone came and tapped her on the shoulder. It was Destiny but in this dream Hope didn't know who Destiny was. "It's okay, you're fine now." Said Destiny.

"Huh? what's going on? What are you talking about" Hope looked at herself, she as covered in dirt. "What happened to me?" she asked. Destiny smiled.

"Just come with me I'll explain on the way." Hope looked at Destiny.

"I don't know you, how can I trust you?" asked Hope. Looks like DT didn't only take what I said, I've heard that trust line in a million books and movies.

"You can trust me. C'mon"

"No I can't, I can't trust anyone anymore"

"Who has hurt you Hope?"

"Everyone."

"But no one"

"I'm sorry?" Now Hope looked confused. What Destiny was saying started to sound like something Hope would say.

"I'm quoting you" said Destiny.

"You are?"

"Yes you said that on January 14, 2010."

"I did?"

"You did" answered Destiny. "Now will you come with me, I know just about everything about you. You can trust me."

"No! How do I know your no some creepy stalker?" asked Hope.

"Because I'm not."

"That doesn't mean anything. I won't come with you! I can't come with "Then all of a sudden there was a light coming out of Destiny's hands. Hope stared at the light she was mesmerized then Hope said "I will follow you." Then Hope followed Destiny as the walked towards the light. Did I just see what I thought I saw? DT gave Destiny some sort of magical power in this dream and Hope gets nothing. They weren't in a dark room anymore, now they were in a bright room but to the other side it was dark. The dark side was the side they came from.

"Hope it's finished." Said Destiny.

"what's finished?"

"You."

"I'm finished?"

"It's what you wanted."

"What are you talking about?

"You were so upset that you just wanted to be finished." Then Hope woke up. That was kind of creepy, was Destiny implying that Hope was dead? That she wanted to be dead? Hope felt her arms, legs and bed just to be sure she was still alive. She let out a deep breathe when she found out that she was all right. I guess that was like symbolism or something, don't you think? I mean Hope went from the dark side which was life to the bright side . . . what's DT trying to say? In my version nothing like that happens.

Destiny's not in it and Hope doesn't die. DT is putting things into Hopes head that shouldn't be there. I think she's trying to expose me to Hope, if she does I'll expose her to Destiny.

Hope went downstairs and to get some orange juice. When she opened the fridge she turned around because she thought she saw something unusual. Hope got scared at the site of someone turned around, the persons arm moved up and came back down then she heard a sort of crunching sound. She shrieked only to find out that, that someone turned around had just been her father eating a cookie. Hope let out a sigh of relief.

"You scared me." Said Hope. Her father smile as if he was proud of himself.

"I scared the unshakable just by eating a cookie? Cool! Or as you kids say, coolio!" he said as he stuffed the remainder of the cookie into his mouth.

"Dad, I don't even talk to those kids and I know they don't say that."

"Whatevs, good night Hopester" replied her father and he went back upstairs.

"Dad, you know I don't like being called that."

"Good night! H dawg" He replied from the top step. He wasn't the coolest when it came to nicknames. Hope turned back around to get some juice, it made me thirsty so I got some too from my kitchen. We tellers live in our own town, we live in the horizon line so we have our own houses, stores, and pet tellers, the pet tellers are actual pets. The sad thing is when they loose a home up here a pet looses home down there. Anyways back to Hope, a few minutes later Hope went back upstairs.

That night Hope heard a lot of coughing. It came from Little J.J's room. He went inside and saw her baby brother coughing hysterically. "Are you okay?" asked Hope. He couldn't answer he just kept coughing, "Okay I guess not. I'll go get you some water" said Hope. Little J.J coughed.

"Mommy said that owange juice is good for a cough" said Little J.J

"Okay then I'll get you some orange juice." She went back downstairs and got a Sippy cup full of juice along with some gummy cough drops. Then Hope went back upstairs to Little J.J's room and he was still coughing. "Here drink this" said Hope handing him the water "But drink slowly so you won't get hiccups and eat these if you start coughing a lot again."

"Okay" Hope put the cough drops on the night stand and fluffed her brother's pillow so he would go back to sleep. Before Hope opened the door Little J.J called out "Thank You" Hope looked over her shoulder and smiled then she left.

It was kind of hard for Hope to fall back asleep. I wanted her to stay awake incase watching her sleep made me fall asleep and that could give DT the chance to come ruin something else. I wonder why she didn't just kill me though when she came in, it's what she wanted to do. I'm not saying I want her to, that'll end Hopes life but I'm just wondering why she didn't.

CHAPTER SEVEN

That morning Hope woke up to the sound of more coughing. It was four A.M and I hadn't notice I fell asleep. I checked through my book nothing was changed. Hope went into Little J.J's room. He was still coughing, his Sippy cup was half full and he used all of his gummy cough drops. "Did mommy or daddy come to check on you yet?" asked Hope while yawning.

"Yes. Mommy said she'll make a doctor appointment and daddy brought me some more juice." Little J.J held up his Sippy cup to show Hope.

"Okay that's good"

"Nooo my thwoat is itchy"

"Drink some juice then it'll probably stop the itchiness."

"Okie Dokie Ravioli!"

"You've been hanging out with dad haven't you?" asked Hope. Little J.J giggled. Hope left the room.

"Hope has left the building" called out Little J.J. Yea he's definitely been spending a lot of time with their dad, like father like son.

"Hope!" called out her mother. She was spotted from the hallway. "Come in!" She went into her parents room. Her dad was still sleeping but her mom was wearing her work clothes.

"why are you getting ready this early?" asked Hope.

"I have to go to work now because well you know my boss' daughter Marissa?"

"The one who loses everything?"

"Yea"

"She taking over for the week and lost the papers I sent her and the file is on my work computer so I have to resend it to her by six which is the deadline she gave me since she has to give in all the papers of all the employees working on this project by noon." I've seen Marissa and she could be their Aunt Tecla's daughter

"Oh well that sounds like it sucks"

"anyways do you mind walking to school with your brother?"

"but he's sick! He'll get worse!"

"You're his big sister, you have the responsibility to make sure he's all warm and toasty, thanks sweetie" her mom gave her a kiss on the forehead and left after saying by to Little J.J and leaving a note for their dad. The worse part about this was that Hope's mom dropped Destiny off too and now she had to walk with them since neither of her parents were able to drive her to school. Destiny's mom's license was suspended because of this whole thing with speeding and yelling at the cops, and her dad went to work pretty early.

Their dad left at six A.M every day and came back four, so Hope and Little J.J were alone after six. Them being alone was like a nightmare for Hope, she had to do so much. First both of them brushed their teeth and Little J.J kept asking her to do stuff that their mom would do like dance while brushing their, Hope refused to do that so instead she just watched him dance. Hope also had to put out Little J.J's clothes and get his jacket, gloves and all that stuff ready for him.

The hardest part was breakfast, there was nothing in the fridge and they didn't even have cereal. That was one of the hard parts about having parents who were always working, even though their dad comes home at four he works on the computer until eight or sometimes even later. It was kind of sad because that was one of the reasons that caused Hope's sadness. Hope knew she had like six or seven dollars in her backpack they were going to go get some breakfast from the coffee shop they pass on their way to school. It has a few thing they could eat and occasionally when they had no breakfast at home their mom would take them there to grab a bite.

Little J.J was the one who had to tell Destiny they had to walk and that they were going to get food at the coffee shop. He was all bundled up thanks to Hope but was still coughing. Hope and Destiny didn't look at each other very much, they avoided talking. The only person who really talked was Little J.J then Destiny and Hope just replied to what he said.

"Sissy I'm tired can you carry me?" asked Little J.J.

"We're only like two blocks away." Said Destiny.

"Yea I can see the coffee shop from here." Said Hope. Little J.J made a puppy dog face.

"That doesn't work on me." Said Hope "Now hold my hand we have to cross the street."

"Pleaseeee" asked Little J.J.

"Fine, but only as far as the coffee shop." Hope picked up Little J.J and they walked across the street. He was happy now but was very heavy to Hope because of his jacket and backpack.

"Here I'll take the backpack." Said Destiny when she saw that Hope was struggling to carry him.

"Thanks" said Hope. Those were the first words they've said to each other since the little incident yesterday. Little J.J smiled when he saw them actually look at each other while speaking. The three went 1 more block and finally got to the coffee shop, but as they were going they saw Destiny. They went inside and looked up at the menu. The prices weren't too high but the food wasn't too big either, everything was kind of tiny. Destiny went up to the register and bought a glazed croissant with her own money.

"Little J.J what do you want?" asked Hope. He stared at the menu. Hope stared at it too then she bought a fruit cup and an iced tea. Honestly none of the stuff here looked good enough to have as breakfast, it wasn't enough food. Little J.J wanted the big soft pretzel so Hope bought him that, then the three walked all the way to school.

"Bye Sissy" said Little J.J when Hope was about to drop him off, that girl Mindy heard him.

"Bye Sissy" said Mindy laughing. A few other kids pointed and laughed with her.

"Leave her alone!" shouted Destiny. Wow Destiny's been doing a lot of shouting these few days.

"It's okay" said Hope.

"She says that because she's a sissy!" said Mindy laughing. Mindy and the others walked away leaving only Hope and Destiny.

"Listen Hope," said Destiny, "I was wrong you were right and I'm really sorry"

"Okay"

"so you forgive me?"

"Yea, I guess." Destiny smiled and walked to class. Hope however, still had to go to see the guidance counselor because of what happened yesterday. When Hope got close to Ms. C's room Destiny came running.

"Hope!" yelled Destiny "I forgot to tell you something!"

"What is it?" asked Hope. Destiny waved the hall pass in her hand as she tied to catch her breathe.

"I forgot to tell you that I told Ms. C about the dream" said Destiny.

"What about the dream?"

"Everything, oh and I had another dream that you were in, we'll talk at lunch okay? Well bye" Hope was in they didn't agree not to tell anyone.

"Wait." Said Hope, "Why did you tell her?"

"Because you said a therapist could tell us what I means." Destiny was right but still who tells stuff like that to Ms. Crazy Is Good?

"She's not a therapist, she's some lady who doesn't think into life!"

"Hope!" called out Ms. C.

"Wait Hope did you have another dream yesterday too?"

"Yea . . ." said Hope, she sounded worried.

"Great I wanted to talk about it, well bye now!" Sometimes Destiny was kind of corny. Hope walked in, she was nervous because she didn't want to talk about the dream. The rainbows and sunshine still made Hope sick. "Would you like some candy?" Ms. C didn't look as annoyed at Hope as she did yesterday it was like she was a whole other person, so calm and so awkward. Hope took out a piece of gum from the jar of various candies. "I heard about the dream" She said "from your friend Destiny, she is your friend right?"

"Yea she's my friend." Said Hope not making any eye contact.

"Just asking because I don't see you with many kids."

"are you saying I don't have friends?"

"Why no it's just-"

"Stop, it's true I don't, I think I've taken up enough of your time, Goodbye." Hope got up from the chair.

"But Hope I want to help"

"You can't fix everything"

"I can try to" Ms. C probably did want to help, but I didn't want it.

"You have tried, everyone has but I've fell and it didn't hurt, I've drowned but I didn't die, many things have happened but all I did was cry." Replied Hope.

"You can talk about all that here."

"Talking just lets out a noise from your body it's safer to stay unspoken" said Hope and she walked right out of the room not looking back. I think Ms. C got confused again. It's funny when she gets confused.

CHAPTER EIGHT

L unch wasn't too disgusting that day. They had peanut butter sandwiches and cheese sandwiches. Hope's school wasn't the richest school ever. Destiny was eager to talk about the latest dream, and you know what I just noticed? The dream DT wrote for Hope was also given to Destiny. We tellers are kind of slow, the only school we went to was training for becoming a teller. Destiny had a handful of questions, her eagerness was kind of annoying.

"Okay so I was some sort of angel or magical being in this dream right?" asked Destiny. Hope felt uncomfortable talking about this particular dream, it was embarrassing for Hope too tell Destiny it scared her, well it scared me but I'm her, well not really, but still I don't want to talk about it. You didn't watch it and your not apart of it, that's why you might think I'm over exaggerating or something, but DT is really scary me. I don't know what she's planning to but she's giving Hope dreams that are saying that she dead. Hope can only die if I sign for her to die because I want to retire or if I die myself and the other day DT did try to kill me. DT is trying to use Destiny to get to Hope to get to me to get me back.

"It's kind of foggy now." Said Hope. DT knew she was lying, I could see it through Destiny.

"Okay . . . hey can I see your writing journal?" asked Destiny.

"Why?" Hope didn't like it when people read her notebook.

"Just to see it."

"Sorry it's just that I don't like it when people read my notebook."

"Oh okay I get it." Said Destiny, she understood that was a no. The rest of lunch was pretty quiet, it gave me time to think of a plan. So this is what I thought of: I'm going to sneak in into DT's house and go through her book. I'm going to take the dream she wrote for Destiny and give it to Hope like she did to me, then I'll call the council when I see her coming and then she'll be taken away before she can hurt me. Good plan huh?

So that evening I got to her house and sneaked in through the back door when she left. I looked through the book for tonight's dream, Hope wasn't in it so I took DT's pen and wrote Hope in. Next I copied the story on to my book and left discreetly. Now she'll have her payback for trying to kill me. It'll be over for Destiny if I hurt her teller, but nothing will happen to Destiny if DT's locked up. I'm confident that this will work, just have to try not to jinx anything.

That night was the big night, it was dream night. The dream started off with Hope and Destiny, they were simply hanging out in Hope's room doing homework. "I'm thirsty" said Hope.

"Me too." Replied Destiny.

"Let's get some iced tea."

"Yay! Homework break!" Exclaimed Destiny.

"The joy will soon bring despair" said Hope. Then the two girls left to go to the kite nut when they left the room they were no longer in Hope's house. Now they were somewhere else. In sight were a few trees, an ocean, and a cave. It melt like rotten fish and you could hear a faint noise, it was music.

"wow where are we?" asked Destiny, "Did you put a spell on us or something?"

"I didn't do anything now Shhh. Listen" said Hope. They walked towards the sound.

"It's coming from the cave." Said Destiny. They walked closer towards the cave. Destiny stayed behind Hope, she was scared and was willing to risk Hope's life for hers. Some friend she was. Then they saw a little girl who was about a few years older than Little J.J maybe more. She was singing and didn't see Hope or Destiny. The song was acoustic and a little sad but she had a really good voice for a little girl. It went like this:

Trapped inside a cage in the middle of the night
Why am I always wrong but they always have to be right
It's not fair
But I don't care
Just get me out of here!
Just get me out
Just get me out
Just get me out of here
I lied a thousand times to open their eyes

I dreamt a thousand dreams just to realize
Everything
But-

That's when she saw Hope and Destiny.

"Who are you?" She asked pulling a pocket knife out of her pocket and held it up in front of her. She was so small it was hard to think that she'd really have one of those. It would actually make more sense if Hope or Destiny had one instead, but oh well who said dreams had to be practical.

"Calm down, we just want to know where we are." Said Destiny. Hope walked forward towards the little girl, Destiny stayed where she was with her hands up as if she was going to be arrested.

"Stand back, I'm not afraid to use this." Said the little girl.

"And I'm not afraid of you." Replied Hope, Destiny coughed as a warning for Hope to stop talking and before they knew it that little girl was running towards Hope and she kicked her leg. It didn't affect Hope too badly but Destiny was scared. "Don't let that little red mark you left on my leg flatter you, I've been hurt worse." Said Hope looking straight into the girl's eyes.

"Listen" said Destiny, "Can you please just tell us where we are? We don't want to disturb you so if you could just tell us we'll leave."

"You're no where." Said the little girl.

"But everywhere?" asked Hope. The little girl looked surprised.

"Yes." She answered. Hope looked at Destiny, Destiny looked completely lost.

"This is unspoken." Said Hope.

"What are you talking about." Asked Destiny.

"You'll know soon." Said the little girl, "By the way my name is Butterfly." Hope and Destiny looked at each other.

"Is that a real name?" asked Destiny.

"It is." Said Butterfly.

"But it's not" said Hope she actually sounded happy.

"Yes." Said Butterfly. Hope looked around the cage and noticed her drawings, drawings by other people and famous drawing, they just appeared as Hope turned around.

"What are all these pictures?" asked Hope still looking around.

"Here we hold everything and nothing. That's why they weren't here before then appeared, next you will see different things." Answered Butterfly. Then it all goes into a black hole." Answered butterfly.

"Black hole?" asked Hope.

"Yes sometimes I go into the black hole just for fun. Do you want to try it'll be here in a little less than five minutes?" Said Butterfly.

"Black hole? Don't you like never come back when you go through a black hole?" Asked Destiny. Butterfly giggled.

"Just wait" she said. A few minutes later there was a harsh wind that blew everything away. "Wait and when I say go jump up!" screamed Butterfly over the wind. Then there was voice, an electronic voice that counted down from twenty, when the voice got to ten Butterfly took Hope and Destiny's wrist and she shouted "Jump!" The three went with the wind and into a hole. When they went through

Destiny laughed, the black hole was a swirly slide, Little J.J could have gone through it. Hope felt as if she was finally home. And that's where it all ended. Telling probably took just a little why but really that dream lasted a couple of hours, and I'm tired so nighty night can't wait to see DT get locked up tomorrow so I need my energy. This plan was the best plan I've had and it's working too, DOUBLE SCORE!

I woke up to a pain. I screamed at the sight of DT standing over me. That pain was her slowly slicing through the layers of skin on my neck. She dropped the knife when I screamed because she was cutting so carefully, it fell on to the handle of the chair then the floor. "What are you doing." I asked.

"Don't ask questions you already know the answer to, it just makes you sound plain dumb." Answered DT, she was right about that one. I kicked her stomach causing her to fall to the floor and I ran to my kitchen where the phone was. I started to dial the counselors but DT was still able to walk and she ran in once I put the phone to my ear, I grabbed a pot and hit her head with it but at that moment she stabbed my arm with the knife. I let out a cry and held my bleeding arm with the knife still in it. She pulled out knife so fast causing my fingers to bleed. I tried to run again but she had already caught me. I did my best to fight her but she fought me back.

"Stop it!" I screamed.

"You first!" She screamed back, "If you just listened this wouldn't have happened." and that's when she really got me. The knife pierced through my neck, I couldn't breathe and I felt myself slowly falling but as I fell my foot pulled

DT's leg causing her to fall as well. She fell so fast and the hardness of the tile floor resulted in the end of DT too. I was crying but I didn't know for what, was it for me or DT? The room was slowly fading in blackness, I couldn't speak my final words, I died Unspoken.

CHAPTER NINE

Now the pain and suffering from that harsh death ended. I'm now retired because my death caused Hope to die. Now It's Hope turn to decide to become a teller or join me up here. Whatever she chooses I hope she could meet me some day. That's right, I died before I became a teller, it's a long story, and that's why I didn't want to fight with DT, I didn't want it to happen again. Now Hope can live in the horizon for a while.

I don't want to leave you wondering might as well tell you what happened with the others. When Hope's parent's realized Hope died they called the police and everybody, they were so upset because the last night they had with her, they ignored her. It was painful for them as they canceled work and sat beside Hope's bed crying all over each other Little J.J walked into Hope's room when her parents were in there and they told him. He understood something was wrong before they told him. Little J.J cried for hours screaming, "SISSY!" it was so sad he was such a great little brother. Hope's parents couldn't stand the thought that she was actually gone, she seemed distant before but now it seemed like she was closer than ever when she really was farther than she could ever go.

Destiny's parents called everyone and the police too just as Hope's parents did. They took it really hard considering their only other child is twenty-eight and moved out three years ago, Destiny was the only one they had to call their little baby.

But you want to know what everyone was wondering? Everyone was wondering how in the world did these two girls both die in their sleep on the same day? Some say it was a coincidence they were both friends. People assumed suicide and talked to the guidance counselor about what they've said to her. Later they found out there was nothing in or out of their bodies that could have killed them. No one knew what had happened.

What really upsets me is that no one ever got the chance to truly understand Hope. Everyone saw her as just that gothic girl but no one knew what she was hiding. No one knew about her tears, no one understood. They all worried about themselves and no one knew about the pain of being all alone. They say she likes to be alone, but really it's only because she's used to it.

People felt bad for the two families so they brought over gift baskets, toys for little J.J, some scented soaps and more, but it didn't help. The two families couldn't forget it with gifts. To me it was like they were bribing the families to be happy because they were sick of seeing them sad if that really was the case then that's just plain wrong.

Everyone who picked on Hope like Mindy or that other kid in her class all felt bad for what they did. It left a scar on everyone. Do you remember what I said before? *You'll figure out more as you go. Follow the clues and it will show. Dreams do end in the morning but don't forget, they begin at night.* The clues lead to this, a dead end, and a dead end is exactly what you needed to find because a dead end is everything and nothing.

Epilogue

Five years later everything was back to normal. Every year on that day that Hope and Destiny became part of the deceased people mourn. Many, many people mourn. The parents, the siblings, the haters. Other than on that day everyone seemed to be normal. Little J.J however changed, he couldn't get over the fact that hi sister wasn't ever coming back. All of Hopes things were moved into the attic but he held on to all her drawings, books, and he couldn't help but invade her privacy, he read her diary. It wasn't exactly a diary really, though it was full of her writing about herself. Little J.J even ripped out a page that she wrote on and he kept it folded neatly under his mattress. On that page was something very special, it was a poem about what could have been and what had actually happened.